CENGAGE Learning

# Novels for Students, Volume 31

Project Editor: Sara Constantakis Rights Acquisition and Management: Jennifer Altschul, Margaret Chamberlain-Gaston, Leitha Etheridge-Sims, Kelly Quin Composition: Evi Abou-El-Seoud Manufacturing: Drew Kalasky

Imaging: John Watkins

Product Design: Pamela A. E. Galbreath, Jennifer Wahi Content Conversion: Katrina Coach Product Manager: Meggin Condino © 2010 Gale, Cengage Learning

For product information and technology assistance, contact us at **Gale Customer Support, 1-800-877-4253.**

For permission to use material from this text or product, submit all requests online at **www.cengage.com/permissions.**

Further permissions questions can be emailed to **permissionrequest@cengage.com** While every effort has been made to ensure the reliability of the information presented in this publication, Gale, a part of Cengage Learning, does not guarantee the accuracy of the data contained herein. Gale accepts no payment for listing; and inclusion in the publication of any organization, agency, institution, publication, service, or individual does not imply endorsement of the editors or publisher. Errors brought to the attention of the publisher and verified to the satisfaction of the publisher will be corrected in future editions.

*Gale*
27500 Drake Rd.
Farmington Hills, MI, 48331-3535

ISBN-13: 978-1-4144-4169-6
ISBN-10: 1-4144-4169-X
ISSN 1094-3552

This title is also available as an e-book.
ISBN-13: 978-1-4144-4947-0
ISBN-10: 1-4144-4947-X
Contact your Gale, a part of Cengage Learning sales
representative for ordering information.

Printed in the United States of America
1 2 3 4 5 6 7 14 13 12 11 10

# *Cold Sassy Tree*

## Olive Ann Burns 1984

## Introduction

Olive Ann Burns's *Cold Sassy Tree*, published in 1984, is a poignant and comic coming-of-age novel set in Cold Sassy, Georgia, in the years 1906 and 1907. It is told in the first person from the point of view of Will Tweedy, who is fourteen years old when the novel's action begins, although he is narrating the story from a more adult perspective in 1914. The novel centers on the scandal caused when Will's grandfather and mentor, Rucker Blakeslee, suddenly marries a much younger woman, Miss Love Simpson, just weeks after the death of his first wife. Will observes the community's reaction to the marriage, the deaths of his grandmother and ultimately his grandfather, and changes in the town brought by modern conveniences and new attitudes. He examines the nature and source of prejudice, ponders the role of God in the lives of individuals, and develops a more mature, adult perspective on life.

# Author Biography

Olive Ann Burns was born on a farm in Banks County, Georgia, on July 27, 1924, the youngest of four children. Because of hardship caused by the Great Depression, her father had to sell the farm, which had been in the family for generations, and move to the small town of Commerce, Georgia, which became the model for the town of Cold Sassy. She attended school in Commerce and later went to high school in Macon, Georgia. She enrolled at Mercer University in Macon, which she attended for two years. She then transferred to the University of North Carolina in Chapel Hill, graduating with a journalism degree.

Burns was originally a journalist. After completing college in 1946, she took a job as a staff writer for the *Atlanta Journal and Constitution* magazine, which later became the *Atlanta Journal* magazine. She held this job for ten years until she married in 1956 and gave birth to two children. She continued, though, to work as a freelance journalist, and until 1967 she wrote an advice column under the name Amy Larkin for the *Atlanta Journal Magazine* and the *Atlanta Constitution* newspaper.

The genesis of *Cold Sassy Tree* came in 1971, when Burns's mother was diagnosed with cancer. Burns decided to begin accumulating materials for a family history and relied on her mother for stories about the family's past. After her mother died in

1972, Burns turned to her father for his recollections of life in Commerce. She discovered that her grandfather had remarried just three weeks after the death of his first wife. A fictionalized version of this story became the premise of *Cold Sassy Tree*, which Burns began writing in 1975 after she herself was diagnosed with cancer. She worked on the novel until it was published in 1984. The book was an immediate success, and in 1985 the American Library Association named it a best book for younger readers.

During the final years of her life, Burns worked on a sequel to *Cold Sassy Tree*. In 1987, however, she was again diagnosed with cancer. The effects of chemotherapy consigned her largely to her bed for the last three years of her life. During those years she dictated *Leaving Cold Sassy* to a neighbor. The novel remained unfinished, but the thirteen chapters Burns completed were published in 1992, two years after her death on July 4, 1990.

## *Chapters 1-4*

In 1914, the novel's narrator, Will Tweedy, recalls events in Cold Sassy, Georgia, that took place primarily in the summer of 1906, when he was fourteen years old. On the night of July 5 that year, Will's grandfather, Rucker Blakeslee, arrives at Will's home to have a drink of corn whiskey; Rucker's wife, Mattie Lou, had never allowed him to keep whiskey in the house. But Mattie Lou has been dead for three weeks. Rucker asks Will to gather his mother, Mary Willis, and his aunt, Loma Williams. When the women arrive, Rucker makes a startling announcement: he is going to marry Miss Love Simpson, a hat maker who works at the general store he owns and who is young enough to be his daughter. Loma reminds Rucker of Mattie Lou's recent death, but Rucker's only reply is, "Well, good gosh a'mighty! She's dead as she'll ever be, ain't she? Well, ain't she?" After Rucker leaves, the two women express their outrage. Miss Love is a Yankee (a northerner), and the marriage will disgrace the family in the eyes of the town.

Will reflects on what has just happened. He recalls that Rucker lost a hand in a sawmill accident and that he needs someone to look after him. He thinks about mourning and reflects that there is a difference between being "in mourning" and actually mourning the loss of a loved one. He worries that his mourning clothes will prevent him from going fishing and taking part in other boyish activities. His reflections are interrupted when his father, Hoyt Tweedy, arrives to announce that Rucker and Miss Love have gone off to get married. Will then thinks about his grandfather, a quick-tempered, domineering old Confederate. He also thinks about Miss Love, whom he has always liked. Miss Love is unlike most of the women in Cold Sassy. She is pretty, wears colorful clothing, and designs fashionable hats. She advocates the right of women to vote. Will believes that Aunt Loma does not like Miss Love because she is jealous of Miss Love's good looks. Finally, he reflects that he does not like his aunt Loma, who married Campbell "Camp" Williams to spite Rucker, her father, after he refused to allow her to pursue an acting career.

## Chapters 5-10

This group of chapters looks back at events surrounding Mattie Lou's death. Will thinks about his grandmother and her passion for gardening. He remembers that her final illness began with a stroke. During her illness, Rucker took good care of her, but the only family member he allowed to visit her was Will. One day, Will stole into the room but backed out because his grandfather was crying. Later, Rucker appeared in the room with one of Mattie Lou's roses as a reminder of their courtship. He asked Will to pray with him. In his prayer, Rucker asked God to forgive his sins against Mattie

## Media Adaptations

- A 1989 film version of *Cold Sassy Tree*, starring Faye Dunaway, Richard Widmark, Frances Fisher, and Neil Patrick Harris (as Will Tweedy) and directed by Joan Tewkesbury, was released by Turner Home Entertainment in 1990 and rereleased in 1998. Running time is 97 minutes.

- A comic opera version of the novel was written by Carlisle Floyd and produced by the Houston Grand Opera Orchestra and Chorus. It was released as an audio CD by Albany Records in 2005.

- An audiobook version of *Cold Sassy*

*Tree*, read by Tom Harper, was released by Audiofy/Blackstone in 1993 and rereleased by Playaway in 2008. The reading runs thirteen hours.

---

Mattie Lou's condition seemed to improve, but a week later it worsened, and she had hallucinations as Will sat by her bed. That night, she died, and Rucker seemed heartbroken. Mattie Lou had treated Miss Love with kindness when the younger woman was ill with the flu, so Miss Love wanted to return the kindness and cleaned the house for Rucker. On the morning of the funeral, Rucker asked Will to help him gather all of Mattie Lou's roses. The two then took the roses to Mattie Lou's grave, which they lined with a bed of roses. The day after the funeral, Rucker returned to work at his store, but he treated everyone coldly. Will's recollection of past events concludes with the town's Fourth of July parade. No U.S. flags were in evidence; all of the flags were Confederate Civil War flags. Participants in the parade included Civil War veterans, who normally would have been led by Rucker. However, Rucker declined to take part because of Mattie Lou's death.

## *Chapters 11-16*

This group of chapters details Will's near-death experience on the town's railroad tracks. He decides that because Rucker has gotten married, the mourning period must be over, so he decides to go fishing. He takes along with him his dog, T.R., named after President Teddy Roosevelt. To get to the fishing creek, he has to pass through Mill Town, the area of Cold Sassy where poor laborers at the cotton mill live. Although the mill is a major contributor to the town's economy, people look down on Mill Town residents, calling them "lintheads." Will has feelings for one of Mill Town's residents, Lightfoot McClendon, a girl in his class at school. Will hopes that he does not run into Hosie Roach, a much older boy from school who fights Will.

On impulse, Will decides to cross the train trestle over the creek. When he is halfway across, though, a train comes. As Will is about to dash to safety, his fishing pole becomes entangled. He lies down on the railroad bed between the tracks, and the train passes over him. Lightfoot appears to help him off the tracks. The train stops, and Will boards it to ride back to town. Back home, everyone is elated by Will's escape. A crowd gathers at his home to talk about the incident, recall past train wrecks, and gossip about the marriage of Rucker and Miss Love. Rucker appears, and in the kitchen, Will tells Rucker about the train incident. The two then have a discussion about God's will and the power of prayer. Rucker asks the family and guests to join him in prayer, astonishing them by asking God to help Miss Love realize that any good in him was because of Mattie Lou. Everyone hugs Miss Love except Loma, who leaves in a jealous huff.

# Chapters 17-20

These chapters include hints of Will's adolescent development and his growing relationship with Miss Love. Will has a dream in which Lightfoot takes off her clothes just before being hit by a train. In the same dream, he sees himself running from the train, but his path is blocked by Aunt Loma. After Will awakens, he remembers why he hates Aunt Loma. His aunt is only six years older than he is, and when they were children they played together. But on Loma's twelfth birthday, she broke all of his lead soldiers. He thinks of other people he hates, including his Grandfather Tweedy, a lazy farmer who does little more than spout religion from his porch.

Will goes to Rucker's house to help Miss Love clean and go through Mattie Lou's things. Before he announces his arrival, he watches Miss Love playing the piano and is aroused by the sight of her figure. He discovers that Miss Love has her own bedroom, so he concludes that her marriage with Rucker is a marriage of convenience. Rucker arrives and allows Miss Love to give him a haircut and shave off his beard. Will is then struck by how alike he and Rucker look. Later, Will asks Miss Love why she married his grandfather. He thinks that Miss Love will be offended by the question, but she is not. She replies that she married Rucker to keep house for him. In exchange, Rucker has promised to leave her the house and some money. The two also discuss Miss Love's former boyfriend, Son Black. Will asks why she did not marry him; she replies that she has decided not to marry because of something bad that had happened to her in Texas, though she does not say what. Cold Sassy's town gossips believe that she rejected Black because he had gotten Miss Love's best friend pregnant.

## Chapters 21-27

A cowboy appears, who turns out to be Clayton McAllister, another of Miss Love's old boyfriends. A neighborhood gossip, Miss Effie Belle Tate, sees McAllister kissing Miss Love passionately. Rucker arrives, and surprisingly, the two men get along. Rucker invites McAllister to spend the night, but McAllister declines. He leaves behind a saddle as a present for Miss Love. Rucker tells her that if she wants to marry McAllister, he would be willing to annul their own marriage. He asks her whether she would like to have a horse, and when she brightens at the prospect, Rucker sends Will to fetch a horse from a cousin in the country. Will decides to combine the errand with a camping trip. He visits his Grandpa Tweedy to borrow a wagon to use on the trip, which turns out to be a disaster. On the way back home, he makes up stories about his aunt Loma. After the stories are spread around town, Rucker scolds Will. Meanwhile, Miss Love has been removed from her position as piano player in the church because of her presumed improper behavior.

## Chapters 28-31

Everyone in town knows about the nature of Rucker and Miss Love's marriage. Mary Willis tells Will that while Will was camping, Miss Love herself announced in the store where she works that she and Rucker were sleeping separately. This revelation is further evidence to the town that Miss Love married Rucker for his money. Loma's resentment of Miss Love grows after Loma and her husband, Camp, visit Rucker's house to lay claim to Mattie Lou's piano and other items. Miss Love refuses to relinquish them. Will concludes that Miss Love has declared war on the family.

Will's friendship with Miss Love continues to grow as he goes to Rucker's house to help her train her horse. In their conversation about Queenie, the Tweedys' black cook, Will learns that some of his assumptions about Queenie's position may be untrue and naive and that she is the victim of racism. Will goes to Loma's house to apologize for the stories that he told about her. There he is dismayed by how poorly she treats her husband. He is astonished to discover that she found the stories funny, and the two of them actually get along during the afternoon. Loma gives Will a journal and urges him to write, but Will is resolved to become a farmer.

## Chapters 32-35

Rucker has offered Hoyt and Mary Willis tickets for a trip to New York. Mary Willis is reluctant to go, still mourning the death of Mattie Lou. Just as she changes her mind, though, Rucker announces that he and Miss Love are going to use the tickets to go to New York to buy stock for the store. Rucker invites the entire town to a church service at his house. He invites Loomis, Queenie's husband and an employee at the store, to preach at the service. Hoyt declines to attend the regular Sunday service at the Presbyterian church, which mystifies everyone until he appears on Sunday morning with a new Cadillac, the first automobile in Cold Sassy. After practicing driving for a week, Hoyt and Will offer rides to the townspeople, but Hoyt pointedly refuses to offer Miss Love a ride.

Miss Love begins to win friends in Cold Sassy. From New York, she sends postcards, telling the women of the dresses she has picked out for them. Will takes Lightfoot for a drive in the car. They park at a cemetery and talk. Lightfoot cries because of the death of her father. She cannot afford a grave marker for him, and her aunt has taken her out of school. Will kisses her passionately, imitating the kiss he saw Clayton McAllister give Miss Love. A nosy townswoman sees them kissing, forces Lightfoot to leave, and lectures Will.

## *Chapters 36-41*

Hoyt learns that Will and Lightfoot have been kissing and punishes Will by whipping him. After Rucker and Miss Love return from New York, Mary Willis invites them for dinner. At dinner, Rucker talks about the New York trip, particularly his newfound interest in automobiles. It also becomes clear that Rucker and Miss Love have become closer during the trip and that their marriage of convenience is evolving into a true marriage. Rucker and Miss Love tell Will that they have bought a car and that they intend to sell cars in Cold Sassy. Miss Love begins to put together a plan for selling the cars. Will is saddened that Lightfoot no longer attends school, but he is surprised that Hosie Roach, his former enemy, has become friendly with him.

Will begins to notice that Rucker and Miss Love are treating each other with a great deal of affection. As the three drive to the county fair, Will feels that he is intruding on them. After an accident that damages the car, the three spend the night at the home of a local family. Will and Rucker share a room, but during the night Will hears Rucker going into Miss Love's room and overhears their conversation. Miss Love rejects Rucker's romantic overtures, saying that she has a secret that would make her repellent to any man. She confesses that when she was twelve, her mother was dying. Her father was a drunk and accused her mother of having an affair. He claimed that Miss Love was not his daughter, and to prove it, he raped her.

## Chapters 42-46

Rucker wins a drawing that allows him to rename the town's hotel. The name he chooses is the Rucker Blakeslee Hotel. Rucker spends more time at home with Miss Love; although he says that he is ill, and indeed has a cough, his appetite is unaffected. He and Miss Love go on buggy rides together and seem to become much closer. Aunt Loma directs the school's Christmas play, but Will plays a practical joke by releasing rats in the school auditorium. He later apologizes to Loma, and he is gratified that his relationship with Loma is back on its old footing of hatred.

Camp sends Loma away on a trip to Athens, Georgia, claiming that he wants to use her absence as an opportunity to fix the plumbing. He asks Hoyt to help him. When Hoyt and Will arrive at Camp's home, they hear a gun blast and discover that Camp, who always felt like a failure, has committed suicide. Some townspeople believe that Camp does not deserve a funeral because he committed suicide, but Rucker arranges a funeral and insists that Camp be buried at Mattie Lou's feet in the family plot. Loma, with her baby, Campbell Junior, moves into Will's home, where she gets help with the baby and uses her time to write plays and poetry. Miss Love's birthday is on Valentine's Day, and to celebrate her birthday, she resolves to get indoor plumbing. Rucker agrees, and in addition he buys her a record player. Rucker hires Hosie Roach to replace Camp at the store and allows Loma to work at the store as a milliner (hat maker). On his fifteenth birthday, Will shaves for the first time. He runs into Lightfoot, who tells him that she is going to marry Hosie.

## *Chapters 47-50*

During a robbery at his store, Rucker is shot. As he is convalescing, Will overhears him conversing with Miss Love about Jesus and whether God answers prayers. He says to Miss Love, "They ain't no gar'ntee thet we ain't go'n have no troubles and ain't go'n die. But a God'll forgive us if'n we ast Him to." They also discuss changing the name of the town to something more up-to-date. Will sees Rucker and Miss Love kissing and concludes that their union is a real marriage. Rucker's condition takes a turn for the worse when he catches pneumonia and begins to hallucinate. Miss Love reveals that she is pregnant with Rucker's child. Later that day, Rucker dies. He has ordered that his funeral be a simple one. He has left his house and some money to Miss Love, and he has divided his other money and property between Mary Willis and Loma, who, Will reflects, are likely to be upset that some of the money will go to Miss Love's child. Rucker has appointed Hoyt manager of the store and left Will money for college that he can collect if he works at the store for ten years.

Miss Love decides to remain in Cold Sassy so that her child can grow up around family. She tells Will that she hopes he can be a father to the child. A month later, the town changes its name to Progressive City. To make room for improvements in the town, the Cold Sassy tree, a sassafras tree, is cut down. People, including Will, take chunks of the tree's roots to make tea. Years later, Will notes that he still has his piece of the tree, along with the newspaper story of the incident on the train trestle; a photo of Rucker, Miss Love, and himself; and a buckeye that Lightfoot gave him as a memento to remember her by.

## *Mattie Lou Blakeslee*

Mattie Lou is Will Tweedy's grandmother and the wife of Rucker Blakeslee. She dies before the novel's action begins and does not appear directly in the story. She was a good wife to Rucker and earned the respect of the town for her kindness. She was an avid gardener and loved her rosebushes.

## *Rucker Blakeslee*

Rucker is a veteran of the Civil War, the patriarch of his family, and the owner of the town's general store, which becomes the hub of gossip. He has a commanding physical presence, and he enjoys shaking up Cold Sassy by violating its norms and defying its conventions, particularly by marrying a much younger woman, Miss Love, just weeks after his first wife's death. He likes to puncture the pretensions and hypocrisies of the townspeople. He is depicted as stubborn, cantankerous, and brash. At the same time, he is more open-minded than most of the people in Cold Sassy, including his own daughters. He is a man of great integrity, and as such he has a profound effect on his grandson, Will Tweedy. He is an intensely religious man, but his religion, unlike that of many of the townspeople, is not just for outward show. Rather, he thinks deeply about spiritual questions. After his beard is shaved off, it is discovered that he and Will bear a marked physical resemblance to each other. The two characters are in a sense mirror images. Will grows and develops by becoming a bit more like his grandfather; Rucker grows and develops by becoming a little more like Will. He becomes more easygoing and less stingy as his marriage to Miss Love grows into one of genuine affection.

## *Aunt Carrie*

Although Will Tweedy refers to this woman as "Aunt" Carrie, she is not his aunt but simply a close family friend. She is regarded as a bit of an oddball, and other than Miss Love, she is the only woman in Cold Sassy who advocates women's suffrage.

## *Loomis*

Loomis, an African American, works at Rucker Blakeslee's general store and is the husband of the Tweedys' cook, Queenie. He is a kind man and is regarded as a good preacher.

## *Clayton McAllister*

Clayton is a rancher from Texas. He is charming, but he treats Miss Love badly; his past treatment of her caused her to resist love and marriage.

## *Lightfoot McLendon*

Lightfoot is a studious girl in Will Tweedy's class at school. She and Will have feelings for each other, but later, after her father dies, she announces to Will that she is marrying Hosie Roach.

## Queenie

Queenie, an African American, works as a cook for the Tweedy family and is the wife of Loomis. She feels the effects of racial prejudice in Cold Sassy.

## Hosie Roach

Hosie is a much older boy who still attends Will Tweedy's school. The two boys are enemies, though the townspeople generally think highly of Hosie. Eventually, Lightfoot McClendon agrees to marry him after he takes a job at Rucker's general store.

## Miss Love Simpson

Miss Love works as a hat maker in Rucker's general store, and she marries Rucker three weeks after his first wife, Mattie Lou, dies. She is depicted as kind, openhearted, exuberant, spirited, and a breath of fresh air in Cold Sassy. Like Rucker, she defies the town's conventions. Questions arise as to the nature of the marriage. Many of the townspeople believe that she marries Rucker for his money. Will suspects that Rucker simply needs someone to take care of him. Questions also arise about whether

Rucker and Miss Love were having an affair before Mattie Lou died. As the novel approaches its climax, though, it becomes apparent that their marriage has developed and deepened. Miss Love's initial resistance to entering into a real marriage is the result of a childhood incident: When she was twelve, she was raped by her drunken father. Her relationship with Will Tweedy, the novel's narrator, is important in depicting the growth of Will's character. He has always liked Miss Love. As the two get to know one another, Will comes to understand her more. His support of Miss Love and the marriage is key to his ability to outgrow the moral and social constraints of Cold Sassy.

## Effie Belle Tate

Miss Tate is Rucker Blakeslee's next-door neighbor. She is representative of the nosiness and narrow-mindedness of the Cold Sassy community.

## Hoyt Tweedy

Hoyt is Will Tweedy's father and Mary Willis's wife. As Rucker's son-in-law, he works at Rucker's general store. He is depicted as a religious man who treats Will with sternness. He is interested in modern technology and buys the first automobile in Cold Sassy.

## Mary Joy Tweedy

Mary Joy is Will Tweedy's younger sister.

## Mary Willis Tweedy

Mary Willis is Rucker Blakeslee's elder daughter, Will Tweedy's mother, and Loma Williams's sister. She is depicted as a nervous woman who is deeply affected by the death of her mother. She leads a very conventional life and shares many of the prejudices of the town.

## Will Tweedy

Will is the novel's narrator and protagonist. He narrates the events of the novel from the perspective of 1914, though the events take place primarily in 1906 and 1907, when he is fourteen years old (he turns fifteen near the novel's end). The novel focuses on Will's growth and development as he passes from childhood to early manhood, marked symbolically by the first time he shaves. The point of view of the novel is complex because Will is telling the story when he is twenty-two years old, but he tells it from the perspective of his adolescent self. Thus he can show and understand his maturation as he deals with a wide range of complex issues: love, death, sexual awakening, prejudice, narrow-mindedness, social constraints, modernization, and the ways of the South in the decades after the Civil War. His physical resemblance to his grandfather, Rucker, helps suggest that the two characters are mirror images whose lives move in opposite directions. Will becomes more like his grandfather by growing braver and more direct; Rucker becomes more like

Will by becoming more youthful and exuberant.

## Campbell "Camp" Williams

Camp is Loma's husband. He works at Rucker Blakeslee's general store. He is depicted as generally incompetent and the object of Rucker and Loma's scorn. He is eventually driven to despair and commits suicide by shooting himself.

## Loma Williams

Loma is married to Campbell Williams. She is Rucker Blakeslee's younger daughter and thus Will Tweedy's aunt. Just twenty years old, she earlier wanted to pursue a career as an actress. She treats Camp poorly, and Will has long hated her. She is bossy, irritable, and given to fits of jealousy, though she encourages Will to become a writer.

## *Death*

Death plays a prominent role in *Cold Sassy Tree*. Before the action of the novel begins, Rucker and Will are faced with the death of Mattie Lou, Rucker's wife. Will himself has a near-death experience when he is caught on a train trestle and the train passes over him as he lies between the tracks. Later in the novel, Lightfoot's father dies; Will's uncle, Campbell Williams, commits suicide; and Rucker is shot during a robbery at the general store and later dies.

These events force Will to contemplate the meaning of death. After his grandmother dies, he reflects on the difference between being "in mourning" for someone's death and actually mourning that person's death. His thoughts that his mourning clothes will prevent him from fishing and other activities reflect an early immaturity, but the deaths of Camp and his grandfather lead to deeper and more dignified reflections on death. It is through Rucker that Will comes to examine death from a religious perspective. Rucker frequently ponders the issue of God's involvement in human affairs and serves as a mentor to Will on such issues. Rucker has concluded that God does not involve himself directly in human matters and that no amount of prayer can persuade God to change his mind about anything, including death. Rather, humans can pray to God for strength to deal with life's hardships. His lessons even rub off on Miss Love. In Chapter 48, for example, Miss Love says to Rucker,

> Tell Will that sometimes God has to say no for our own good, or to teach us something, or show His power. Sometimes it's just not His will to give us a certain thing. Or He wants to test our faith and see if we trust Him no matter what.

While death is depicted as a sad event, it also opens the possibility of renewal and new life. Rucker is able to find happiness with Miss Love, Loma is released from a marriage she hates and is able to write poetry and plays, and Miss Love will give birth to a new baby after Rucker's death. In this sense, death gives rise to new possibilities, just as Cold Sassy "dies" and is "reborn" as Progressive City.

## *Modern Life and Technology*

*Cold Sassy Tree* shows the introduction of more modern ways to the town. Hoyt Tweedy brings to the town its first automobile, a shiny new Cadillac. The car attracts a great deal of interest among the townspeople, most of whom have never even seen a car. Rucker operates an old-fashioned general store, but after his trip to New York, he and Miss Love decide to become auto dealers, and Miss

Love's business acumen is seen as more modern. The cars stand in contrast to the railroad, the older form of transportation that almost kills Will. Many people in Cold Sassy do not have telephones, but many do, and telephone service is spreading. Miss Love decides that for her birthday she wants indoor plumbing in Rucker's house; Rucker agrees, and additionally he buys her a record player—again, something that most people in the town likely have never seen.

These items, though, are only the outward signs of modernity. More important are more modern attitudes. One clear example is the issue of women's suffrage. Miss Love and Aunt Carrie are the only two women in town who support the right of women to vote. In this way they challenge the town's old-fashioned prejudices. Another is the issue of racial prejudice. Will naively assumes that Queenie, the family's African American cook, accepts her position in life, but Miss Love, who comes from outside Cold Sassy, convinces him that his views might be wrong and that Queenie suffers from discrimination. More generally, the relationship between Rucker and Miss Love challenges the old-fashioned attitudes of the townspeople—attitudes that Will Tweedy in part learns to question and outgrow. Will also acquires a deeper religious faith, one based not on rituals and outward show, as represented by his grandfather Tweedy, but on contemplation, God and the relationship between God and humanity.

# Topics for Further Study

- Conduct an interview with someone who has encountered a situation similar to that depicted in *Cold Sassy Tree*. The interview can be held with a relative, a neighbor, a family friend, or anyone else who has encountered prejudice or social taboos in a community, questioned those taboos, and grown as a result. An example might be a grandparent who grew up in a small town or an immigrant who questioned traditional ways in his or her culture. Transcribe your interview and share it with classmates.

- Conduct Internet research on new technology in the United States in the early years of the twentieth century. In particular, search for images of the cars that were being introduced, such as Hoyt Tweedy's new Cadillac, or the telephones that were spreading through the country. Share the results of your search in a PowerPoint presentation that uses as many visuals as possible.

- During the early twentieth century, Jim Crow laws kept African Americans in an inferior position by segregating them and denying them civil rights. Trace the history of Jim Crow laws and write an essay on precisely how African Americans might have been treated in some small southern American towns in the first decade of the twentieth century.

- Miss Love Simpson was a "suffragette," that is, a woman who advocated the right of women to vote. (Today, the term "suffragist" is preferred.) Conduct research into the history of the women's rights movement in the early twentieth century. Who were some of the most prominent suffragists? What actions did they take to change thinking about voting rights? Prepare a time line of key events in the suffrage movement during these years.

- Perhaps the most famous American novel about race relations, small-town prejudice in the American South, and the observations of young people on the issues of social class, gender roles, and similar matters is Harper Lee's *To Kill a Mockingbird*. Read Lee's novel or watch the widely available movie version and report on its similarities to and differences from *Cold Sassy Tree*, focusing on a single aspect of the two stories. Possibilities include the use of humor, the point of view, or the depiction of community attitudes.

---

At bottom, the entire novel depicts a society and culture on the cusp of new ways of thinking brought about by the advent of modern life—by the still new twentieth century. The old Cold Sassy is symbolized by the Fourth of July parade, with its Civil War—era Confederate flags. Cold Sassy still adheres to the traditions and values of the Old South at the time of the Civil War, but those traditions and values are challenged by Miss Love, a northerner. The old Cold Sassy is also symbolized by the sassafras tree; this old town is replaced by a new Cold Sassy, where the tree is cut down to make room for modern improvements and the town's name is changed to Progressive City. However, the old Cold Sassy is not forgotten; Will still has his piece of the tree in 1914, when he tells the story of Cold Sassy and when the world changed forever with the start of World War I.

## *Social Constraints*

Closely related to the theme of modernity is that of social constraints. Cold Sassy is depicted as a closed-minded community where everyone pays attention to everyone else's business and where people have strong feelings about social matters based on prejudice and tradition. When Rucker announces to his daughters that he is going to marry Miss Love, he knows that he is violating these social conventions and does not care. He is going to remarry when he wants to, not when "society" tells him it is acceptable. A counterpoint to Rucker is his daughters Mary Willis and Loma. They object to the marriage not because they believe that Miss Love is wrong for their father but because they believe that the marriage will make the family an object of ridicule in the town. They also worry that the townspeople will think that Miss Love is marrying Rucker for his money. Other characters, such as Effie Belle Tate, are representative of the social constraints of Cold Sassy. She is depicted as nosy, and when she catches Will kissing Lightfoot in the car at the cemetery, she feels compelled to drive Lightfoot away, scold Will, and tell his father what she witnessed. The townspeople believe that it is not proper to have a funeral service for Camp Williams because he committed suicide.

Will, as a young boy, does not understand these social proprieties. He does not understand, for example, why his grandfather cannot marry Miss Love when he wants to—and indeed he cannot understand why it would not have been possible for Rucker to love Mattie Lou and Miss Love at the same time. Will represents the overturning of social constraints: he accepts the marriage of Rucker and Miss Love. Rucker is a product of the past; he is a Civil War veteran. Miss Love is a product of a more modern world. Their marriage and the birth of their baby suggest that old and new can blend, that social constraints can be overcome, and that people such as Will can grow and change to overcome their prejudices. In time, Miss Love becomes more accepted by the townspeople, and her use of the southern dialect "y'all" ("you all") near the end of the novel, unusual for her because she speaks "properly," suggests that she is becoming part of the fabric of the town.

# Point of View

Point of view refers both to the narrator of a work of fiction and to the perspective from which the novel is being narrated. The narrator is Will Tweedy, who narrates the novel from a first-person point of view, that is, from his own perspective using the pronoun "I." The perspective, though, is more complex. At the time of the novel's events, Will is just fourteen years old, though he turns fifteen near the end. As an adolescent, he is not always able to comprehend the implications of the events that he narrates. Thus, rather than having him tell the story from the fourteen-year-old's perspective, Burns makes her narrator older. Thus, Will tells the story in 1914, by which time he would be twenty-two years old. This technique gives Will more of an adult perspective on events. He is still young enough to capture the innocence and incomprehension of the teenager but old enough to understand the meaning of what has occurred and communicate that meaning to the reader. Thus, the novel blends the two perspectives. Some events would have little meaning if they were narrated by the fourteen-year-old, but if the novel had been narrated entirely from the twenty-two-year-old's perspective, it would have lost much of its poignancy, its ability to capture the perceptions of a character who stands at its center and who has to outgrow his more childish perceptions on his road to adulthood.

## *Symbolism*

Symbolism, a device in which something concrete represents something abstract, can be used in fiction in at least two different ways. Sometimes symbolism occurs in the form of symbolic objects. The symbolism of these objects can be universal, but often it is contextual, meaning that the symbolism derives from how the object is framed in the story. Two prominent symbolic objects in *Cold Sassy Tree* are the Cold Sassy tree itself and the automobiles that Hoyt and Rucker acquire. The Cold Sassy tree is the last remaining tree of a grove of sassafras trees. The town's settlers cut down the grove to make room for the town, but one tree remains. The tree then is symbolic of the town itself and its link with the past. However, as the town moves into the more modern age, the tree has to be cut down to make room for improvements. Thus, the town's link with its past, including its traditions and prejudices, is severed. It is not severed entirely, though. Townspeople, including Will, take pieces of the tree, and Will still has his eight years later at the time he tells the story of Cold Sassy.

In the context of *Cold Sassy Tree*, cars become symbolic objects. Until 1906, the town relied entirely on horses and horse-drawn carts and wagons for transportation. The railroad went through town, but even that is beginning to seem old-fashioned, the product of the previous century. Cars, though, are a symbol of modern progress. They point not only to technological change but to changes in attitude as Cold Sassy moves into a modern age with more modern ways of thinking.

Actions, like objects, can have symbolic overtones. Early in the novel, Will is on the railroad trestle that crosses over the creek where he is fishing. A train approaches, and Will is caught on the trestle with no means of escape. He lies down between the tracks so that the train passes over him. Although he emerges unharmed, the experience is frightening and could have led to his death. In the context of *Cold Sassy Tree*, this scene could be regarded as symbolic. Just as Will is caught on the trestle, so too he is caught between two ways of life in Cold Sassy. Will himself becomes a kind of bridge (like the train trestle), connecting these two ways of life. In the process of surviving his passage over the bridge, he becomes a bit of a hero in the town, just as readers may regard him as heroic for safely negotiating his passage into adulthood. This passage is suggested by another symbolic act: Will's shaving for the first time.

## Dialect

Burns uses a great deal of southern dialect, a distinct form of language and grammar particular to a region or community, in *Cold Sassy Tree*. Thus, for example, late in the novel, Rucker says to Miss Love, "They ain't no gar'ntee thet we ain't go'n have no troubles and ain't go'n die. But … God'll forgive us if'n we ast Him to." Translated into standard English, this passage would read, "There isn't any guarantee that we aren't going to have any troubles and aren't going to die. But God will forgive us if we ask Him to." Will even gives the reader a bit of a lesson in Cold Sassy dialect in Chapter 17: "You need to understand that in Cold Sassy when the word 'aunt' is followed by a name, it's pronounced aint, as in Aint Loma or Aint Carrie." Will goes on to provide further examples. The chief purpose of this use of dialect pronunciation and grammar is to add color to the novel. The reader is invited into the Cold Sassy community and can "hear" the characters speaking in their characteristic ways. Cold Sassy thus becomes more real. In contrast, Miss Love, a northerner, speaks more properly, using standard English grammar and pronunciation. Near the end of the novel, though, she uses the phrase "y'all," dialect for "you all" or simply the plural "you." This hint of dialect suggests that she is becoming part of the Cold Sassy community.

# Historical Context

    *Cold Sassy Tree* is one of many works—novels, short stories, and plays—that examine small-town life in the American South, particularly during the early years of the twentieth century. Chief among American writers who chronicled small-town life was William Faulkner, who created a fictional county in Mississippi that he used in many of his novels and short stories. Other American writers who have taken up this theme include Eudora Welty, Flannery O'Connor, Thomas Wolfe, Tennessee Williams, Harper Lee, and many others. One of the most famous novels set in the rural South and written by a southern writer is *Gone With the Wind* by Margaret Mitchell, and certainly no survey of writing about the rural American South can ignore such novels as Mark Twain's *Adventures of Huckleberry Finn*.

    Southern American literature is often considered a distinct genre in American letters. These works tend to be steeped in the past, in a former pastoral age that is imagined to have existed in the agricultural South before the Civil War. The American South was, and to some degree still is, regarded as unique because of its distinct history and culture. In writing *Cold Sassy Tree*, Olive Ann Burns drew on this tradition of southern writing, steeped in a sense of history and uniqueness. Her perspective is not that of 1984, the year of the novel's publication, although the themes of her novel are universal and are just as applicable in 1984 or any year as they would have been at the turn of the twentieth century. Rather, she draws on stories related to her primarily by her parents to reconstruct a historical past. More to the point, in reconstructing this historical past, she illuminates the clash that takes place when that past is confronted with more modern realities.

The roots of this type of historical writing extend back into the nineteenth century. As tensions in America began to mount over the issue of slavery —tensions that culminated in the Civil War— American writers began to explore the unique characteristics of southern culture: its language, its social institutions, its economy, its religion, and others. Many of these works tried to recreate a pastoral idyll, a world where everyone knew his or her place in the social order and where home, family, and particularly the soil were paramount. Many other novels, including Harriet Beecher Stowe's *Uncle Tom's Cabin*, took the opposite tack, emphasizing the horrors of the South's rigid social structure. In the twentieth century, many writers, including Burns, took a comic view of the South. On the one hand, they examined the South with a great deal of affection, recognizing that they themselves were shaped by the cultural institutions of the region. On the other hand, they were well aware of the limitations and peculiarities of southern culture and revolted from it in what Lucinda MacKethan, in *Southern Space*, has called the "revolt from the village" school of writing. Accordingly, they were able to lampoon its rigid social structure, taboos, and traditions, often by creating grotesque characters and situations. Those tales that emphasize the grotesque are often regarded as belonging to a tradition called Southern Gothic. This tradition arose, many scholars argue, because traditional southern culture had allowed few outlets for reasoned protest and disagreement.

That Burns made use of these traditions of southern writing is immediately clear. She lovingly recreates the dialect and unique patterns of speech in her southern small town, whose citizens have a love of oral storytelling. Characters are given odd names, such as Rucker, Lightfoot McClendon, and Hosie Roach; there are no "John Smiths" in her novel. Many of these characters have features that border on the grotesque; Rucker, with his commanding physical presence, his penchant for fighting, and his general brashness, is the central example. Through her depiction of Mill Town and its poverty, Burns reminds readers that the Old South was built on cash crops such as cotton.

The community's rigid social structure— perhaps the most common theme in southern historical literature—is illustrated on virtually every page. Traditional religion is to some degree lampooned through such characters as Will's Grandfather Tweedy, though it must always be recognized that through Rucker and his relationship with Will, a nontraditional, more thoughtful religious outlook is emphasized. Although the Civil War has ended some four decades before, the war and its aftermath are still a felt reality in the community. The Fourth of July parade route is lined with people waving Confederate flags, not U.S. flags. Miss Love is a threat to the community not just because she is an outsider but because she is from Baltimore, and therefore "practically" a Yankee. It is worth noting, too, that after Rucker and Miss Love travel to the big city—New York—thus leaving behind the small town, Rucker shows more affection to Miss Love and to some extent enters the modern world by deciding to become a car dealer, buying Miss Love a record player, and agreeing to the installation of indoor plumbing.

## Compare & Contrast

- **1900s:** Racial prejudice is widespread throughout the nation but especially entrenched in the post-Civil War South. African Americans are segregated and routinely denied their civil rights.

  **1980s:** The condition of African Americans is greatly improved as a result of the civil rights movement and legislation enforcing civil rights.

  **Today:** Prejudice against African Americans continues among some people, but ongoing civil rights gains have led to greater acceptance and less discrimination. The United States elects its first African American president in 2008.

- **1900s:** The movement to grant voting rights to women is gathering steam through the work of such suffragists as Susan B. Anthony and Alice Paul.

  **1980s:** As a result of the Nineteenth Amendment, which was ratified in 1920, women have enjoyed the right to vote for six decades. In 1984, women cast 53 percent of the votes in the presidential election, and Geraldine Ferraro is the first woman ever to run on the ticket of a major political party in a presidential election.

  **Today:** Women continue to make gains in employment, government, and such institutions as the military. In 2008, Hillary Rodham Clinton becomes the first woman candidate to have a legitimate chance to win the U.S. presidential election.

- **1900s:** The United States, particularly in the rural South, is just beginning to enjoy modern technology, including automobiles, indoor plumbing, electricity, and telephone service. Roughly 33,000 cars are produced in the United States in 1906, including 3,500 Cadillacs. Gasoline costs 6 cents a gallon.

**1980s:** Modern plumbing, cars, and telephone and electrical service are commonplace in all but the poorest homes. U.S. auto production is about eight million cars in 1984. Gasoline costs about $1.20 a gallon.

**Today:** A new technological revolution, marked by home computers, wireless Internet, cell phones, digital television, and many other innovations, is changing the way Americans live and work. The United States produces 8.7 million cars in 2008. Gasoline prices temporarily spike to over $4.00 a gallon in 2008.

---

Many writers who follow the traditions of southern writing have taken an ultimately pessimistic view. They regard southern traditions and taboos as so entrenched that they cannot be resisted or overcome. They ultimately swallow the individual and determine the individual's fate. Others take a more optimistic view, emphasizing the epiphanies, or moments of revelation, when characters recognize the realities around them and are capable of change—and of changing others. *Cold Sassy Tree* clearly belongs to the latter camp. Through Will, Burns stresses that historical realities are not imprisoning. And in connection with the child that Miss Love will give birth to, Cold Sassy can become Progressive City.

# Critical Overview

*Cold Sassy Tree* continues to enjoy a wide and enthusiastic audience and has become part of the reading curriculum in some middle schools, high schools, and even colleges. Nevertheless, at the time of its publication and since then, critical reactions to it have been somewhat mixed. Many critics admire the book. Writing in the *Christian Science Monitor*, for example, Ruth Doan MacDougall calls the novel "captivating" and "joyous." A *Publishers Weekly* reviewer cites the novel's "fine characterization and rich detail," concluding that "it hurts to turn that last page." In the *Washington Post*, Jeanne McManus praises the novel highly, calling Will Tweedy a "sophisticated and astute observer of adults" and describing the book as "rich with emotion, humor and tenderness."

Other critics, though, have been more restrained. Writing in the *New York Times Book Review*, Jason Berry calls some of the novel's black characters "preposterous" and faults the book as a "narrative riddled with clichés." Berry does, however, acknowledge that "the author effectively conveys the world view of an adolescent boy." Perhaps the most negative review of *Cold Sassy Tree* was written by Loxley F. Nichols for the *National Review*. Nichols places the novel in the tradition of other writing about the American South, with its mixture of "pride and … insecurity." He argues that "Miss Burns's love of local color, mixed with a certain defensiveness, and edge of uneasiness, leads her to excesses that the reader may find tiresome." As an example, he notes the novel's overemphasis on explanation, on "spelling out the obvious," and he regards Will Tweedy as an "officious commentator who, all too frequently, intrudes unnecessarily to interpret events ... for the reader." He further argues that Burns "overwrites the regional idiom"—that is, relies too heavily on dialect—and that Rucker Blakeslee's homilies are "ponderous."

# What Do I Read Next?

- After *Cold Sassy Tree* was published, the author received many requests for a sequel. Before her death she completed thirteen chapters of *Leaving Cold Sassy* (1992), which examines Will Tweedy's early adulthood and marriage to a schoolteacher. The book contains an extensive biography of Olive Ann Burns.

- *Green Days by the River* (2000) is a novel by Michael Anthony, an author from Trinidad. It tells the story of Shell, a fifteen-year-old boy who, like Will Tweedy, faces confusion as he grows into adulthood, has to make difficult choices, and learns about the people around him.

- Jerry Amernic's *Gift of the Bambino* (2004) is a coming-of-age tale about a boy and his special relationship with his grandfather.

- *America in the 1900s and 1910s* (2005), by Jim Callan, presents a nonfiction portrait of America—its politics, art, and culture—during the years in which *Cold Sassy Tree* is set. The book's audience is young-adult readers.

- "A Rose for Emily" is a short story by William Faulkner, first published in 1930. It is set in a small southern town, where the townspeople are bound by traditional ways and intrude into the business of others.

- Rudolpho Anaya's *Bless Me, Ultima* (1972) is a coming-of-age novel set in a small town in New Mexico during World War II. It tells the story of a young Hispanic boy who encounters death and confronts religious and moral issues. He is caught between his two families: his father's family, made up of untamed nonconformists, and his mother's family, farmers who are quieter and more religious.

- J. D. Salinger's 1951 novel *The Catcher in the Rye* is widely considered one of the best novels of the twentieth century. It is a coming-of-age novel about a disaffected teenage boy, Holden Caulfield. The character's name is widely known as representative of teenage rebellion, but his story is ultimately optimistic.

# Sources

"1906," in *Antique Automobile Club of America*, http://local.aaca.org/bntc/mileposts/1906.htm (accessed May 27, 2009).

Berry, Jason, Review of *Cold Sassy Tree*, in *New York Times Book Review*, November 11, 1984, p. 32.

Burns, Olive Ann, *Cold Sassy Tree*, Ticknor & Fields, 1984.

"China Outperforms U.S. in 2008 Auto Production," in *EE Times Asia*, April 2, 2009, http://www.eetasia.com/ART_8800568569_499495 (accessed May 27, 2009).

"How Groups Voted in 1984," in *Roper Center* Web site, http://www.ropercenter.uconn.edu/elections/how_gr (accessed May 27, 2009).

MacDougall, Ruth Doan, Review of *Cold Sassy Tree*, in *Christian Science Monitor*, December 7, 1984, p. B12.

MacKethan, Lucinda, "An Overview of Southern Literature by Genre: The South's Literatures of Resistance," in *Southern Spaces*, February 16, 2004, http://www.southernspaces.org/contents/2004/macke (accessed April 19, 2009).

McManus, Jeanne, "Southern Comfort," in *Washington Post*, November 25, 1984, pp. 3, 11.

Nichols, Loxley F., Review of *Cold Sassy Tree*, in *National Review*, April 5, 1985, http://findarticles.com/p/articles/mi_m1282/is_v37/a (accessed April 21, 2009).

O'Dell, Jay, "Trucks, Six-cylinder Engines Gain Popularity in 1906-07," *Herald-Dispatch* (Huntington, WV), December 11, 2008, http://www.herald-dispatch.com/news/x1133222293/Trucks-six-cylinder-engines-gain-popularity-in-1906-07 (accessed May 27, 2009).

Purcell, Kim, "Olive Ann Burns (1924-1990)," in the *New Georgia Encyclopedia*, http://www.georgiaencyclopedia.org/nge/ArticlePrin id=h-1230 (accessed April 16, 2009).

Review of *Cold Sassy Tree*, in *Publishers Weekly*, September 21, 1984, p. 90.

Tilton, John, *World Metal Demand: Trends and Prospects*, Resources for the Future, 1990, p. 179.

# Further Reading

Goldfield, David R., *Still Fighting the Civil War*, Louisiana State University Press, 2004.

> This volume surveys the impact that the Civil War had on "southern memory" and its influence on the South in the decades following the war.

Gray, Richard, and Owen Robinson, *A Companion to the Literature and Culture of the American South*, Wiley-Blackwell, 2004.

> This volume is a comprehensive survey of the literature and culture of the American South, with emphasis on literary works, music, art, politics, and social issues.

Loughery, John, ed., *Into the Widening World: International Coming of Age Stories*, Persea Books, 1994.

> This book is a collection of coming-of-age short stories from a wide variety of cultures around the world. The introduction provides insights into the nature and characteristics of coming-of-age fiction.

Millard, Kenneth, *Coming of Age in Contemporary American Fiction*, Edinburgh University Press, 2007.

Millard's book focuses on recent coming-of-age fiction across a range of racial, class, and gender settings.

Otfinoski, Steven, *Coming of Age Fiction*, Chelsea House, 2009.

The writer explores the issue of young-adult coming-of-age novels that have been challenged in schools and public libraries because of their frank portrayal of controversial issues such as drug use and sexuality.

CPSIA information can be obtained
at www.ICGtesting.com
Printed in the USA
BVHW09s1757111018
529911BV00003B/1296/P

9 781375 378161